HOW TO INVEST IN SNEAKERS

How to Invest in Sneakers
Walter the Educator

Silent King Books
A WhichHead Entertainment Imprint

Copyright © 2024 by Walter the Educator

All rights reserved. No part of this book may be reproduced in any manner whatsoever without written permission except in the case of brief quotations embodied in critical articles and reviews.

First Printing, 2024

Disclaimer

The author and publisher offer this information without warranties expressed or implied. No matter the grounds, neither the author nor the publisher will be accountable for any losses, injuries, or other damages caused by the reader's use of this book. Your use of this book acknowledges an understanding and acceptance of this disclaimer.

How to Invest in Sneakers is a little problem solver book by Walter the Educator that belongs to the Little Problem Solver Books Series. Collect them all and more books at WaltertheEducator.com

LITTLE PROBLEM
SOLVER BOOKS

INTRO

In recent years, the sneaker industry has evolved from a niche market for athletic shoes into a massive, multi-billion-dollar global business. Sneakers have transcended their original purpose, becoming cultural symbols, status symbols, and objects of desire. This transformation has given rise to a new form of investing: **sneaker investing**. Savvy collectors and investors have recognized that rare and desirable sneakers can appreciate in value, sometimes dramatically, making them a legitimate investment vehicle.

How to Invest in Sneakers

If you're intrigued by the prospect of investing in sneakers but don't know where to start, this little book will walk you through everything you need to know. We'll cover the basics of sneaker culture, how to identify profitable sneakers, the best ways to buy and sell, and the risks involved in sneaker investing.

How to Invest in Sneakers

The Sneaker Culture and Market Overview

Before diving into the nuts and bolts of sneaker investing, it's essential to understand the broader sneaker culture. Sneakers have long been associated with sports, particularly basketball and running. However, starting in the late 1980s and early 1990s, thanks to figures like Michael Jordan and the rise of hip-hop culture, sneakers began to gain a foothold in the fashion world.

How to Invest in Sneakers

Today, sneaker culture is a blend of fashion, sports, music, and streetwear, with limited-edition releases driving much of the excitement and demand. Sneakerheads (as avid collectors are known) are willing to pay premium prices for rare and limited-release sneakers, sometimes called **grails**. Brands like Nike, Adidas, and Jordan regularly release exclusive sneakers in limited quantities, creating artificial scarcity and fueling demand. In some cases, sneakers can appreciate significantly in value due to their rarity, brand associations, and cultural significance.

How to Invest in Sneakers

The sneaker resale market has grown rapidly, and according to some estimates, it could be worth more than $30 billion by 2030. Platforms like **StockX, GOAT, and Stadium Goods** have emerged as trusted marketplaces for sneaker reselling, giving investors new ways to trade these sought-after commodities. However, not all sneakers are good investments, and successful sneaker investing requires knowledge, research, and strategy.

How to Invest in Sneakers

The Key Drivers of Sneaker Value

When investing in sneakers, it's important to understand the key factors that determine their value. These drivers can help you predict which sneakers are likely to appreciate and guide your buying decisions.

How to Invest in Sneakers

1. Brand and Model

Some sneaker brands and models are more iconic and sought-after than others. For example, Nike, Adidas, and Jordan are among the most popular brands for sneaker investors. Specific models within these brands, such as the **Nike Air Jordan 1, Adidas Yeezy, and Nike Dunk**, are known for their high resale values. Understanding the history and cultural significance of specific models will help you identify shoes that could hold or increase in value.

How to Invest in Sneakers

2. Limited Edition and Collaboration Releases

Sneakers released in limited quantities tend to be more valuable. Companies often release **limited-edition sneakers** through exclusive collaborations with designers, artists, or celebrities. Collaborations, like the **Travis Scott x Nike** or **Virgil Abloh's Off-White x Nike** lines, are often highly sought after due to their scarcity and association with influential figures. The fewer pairs that are available, the higher the resale value is likely to be, especially if the sneaker is aesthetically appealing or has a unique design.

How to Invest in Sneakers

3. Rarity and Scarcity

Like with any collectible, **supply and demand** play a significant role in determining sneaker prices. The rarer a sneaker is, the more valuable it becomes. A shoe released in a very limited run, especially one with significant historical or cultural relevance, will often appreciate in value over time. For instance, sneakers made specifically for an athlete or produced in limited runs (under 1,000 pairs) can command high prices in the resale market.

How to Invest in Sneakers

4. Condition (Deadstock vs. Used)

In the sneaker world, the term **deadstock** refers to a pair of sneakers that have never been worn, typically in their original box. Deadstock sneakers command the highest prices, as they are considered to be in pristine, untouched condition. On the other hand, used sneakers can still be valuable, especially if the model is rare, but they will typically sell for less. **Mint condition** and deadstock status are key for investment-grade sneakers.

How to Invest in Sneakers

5. Cultural Relevance

A sneaker's cultural significance often influences its value. Sneakers worn by famous athletes or celebrities, featured in films or music videos, or associated with significant events tend to become more desirable. For instance, the **Air Jordan 11 "Space Jam"**, famously worn by Michael Jordan in the 1996 movie *Space Jam*, became a highly coveted sneaker due to its cultural impact.

How to Invest in Sneakers

6. Hype and Marketing

Sneaker brands often use **hype-marketing** strategies to create buzz around a release. Sneakerheads follow releases religiously, anticipating the latest drops from their favorite brands. Social media, influencer endorsements, and celebrity appearances can create an overwhelming demand, leading to rapid price increases in the resale market.

How to Invest in Sneakers

How to Start Investing in Sneakers

Now that you have an understanding of what drives the value of sneakers, it's time to learn how to start your sneaker investment journey. The process can be broken down into several steps:

How to Invest in Sneakers

1. Research the Market

Before you start buying sneakers, you need to immerse yourself in the world of sneaker culture. Follow social media accounts and influencers within the sneaker community to stay updated on the latest news and releases. Websites like **Sneaker News, Sole Collector**, and platforms like **Instagram** and **Twitter** are invaluable resources for keeping up with current trends.

How to Invest in Sneakers

Additionally, familiarize yourself with the major resale platforms, such as StockX and GOAT. These platforms provide historical sales data and insights into how the value of specific sneakers has fluctuated over time. This will give you an idea of which sneakers are good investments.

How to Invest in Sneakers

2. Set a Budget

Like any investment, it's important to set a budget before you begin. Sneaker prices can vary widely, from $100 for a general release pair to thousands of dollars for rare collaborations. Establishing a budget helps you focus on attainable investments without overextending your finances.

How to Invest in Sneakers

It's also important to account for additional costs such as shipping fees, authentication services, and seller fees on platforms like StockX and GOAT. These extra expenses can eat into your profits if not considered beforehand.

How to Invest in Sneakers

3. Choose Your Investment Strategy

There are different strategies for investing in sneakers, depending on your goals and risk tolerance:

How to Invest in Sneakers

- **Short-Term Flipping**: This strategy involves buying newly released sneakers and reselling them quickly for a profit. Often referred to as **flipping**, this is common in the sneaker industry, where hype can cause prices to spike immediately after release. However, the market can be volatile, and prices can also drop after the initial hype dies down.

How to Invest in Sneakers

- **Long-Term Hold**: In this strategy, you buy sneakers and hold onto them for months or even years in hopes that they will appreciate in value over time. Long-term holds typically involve more iconic, limited-edition sneakers that are likely to retain cultural relevance for years.

How to Invest in Sneakers

- **Diversified Portfolio**: Some sneaker investors prefer to take a diversified approach, buying a mix of short-term and long-term sneakers. This helps spread out risk while maximizing potential gains.

How to Invest in Sneakers

4. Secure Your Purchases

Once you have identified which sneakers you want to invest in, the next step is to secure your purchases. This is often the most challenging part, as limited-edition sneakers tend to sell out within minutes of release. To improve your chances of securing rare pairs, consider these tips:

How to Invest in Sneakers

- **Raffles**: Many sneaker retailers hold online or in-store raffles for limited-edition releases. Sign up for as many raffles as possible to increase your chances.

How to Invest in Sneakers

- **Sneaker Bots**: Some sneaker investors use **bots**—software designed to automate the checkout process on retail websites. While this can increase your chances of buying a sneaker before it sells out, bots are controversial and banned by some retailers.

How to Invest in Sneakers

- **Retailer Apps**: Many brands, like Nike and Adidas, release sneakers through their own mobile apps. For example, Nike uses the **SNKRS** app to release many of its exclusive sneakers.

How to Invest in Sneakers

If you miss out on the initial retail release, don't worry. You can still purchase the sneakers on resale platforms, although you'll likely have to pay a premium.

How to Invest in Sneakers

5. Store and Protect Your Investment

Once you've acquired a pair of investment sneakers, proper storage is crucial to maintaining their value. Here are some key tips:

How to Invest in Sneakers

- **Avoid Wearing Them**: If you're investing in sneakers for resale, they should remain deadstock. Wearing the sneakers will significantly reduce their value.

How to Invest in Sneakers

- **Use Climate-Controlled Storage**: Sneakers, particularly those made with leather or suede, can be sensitive to temperature and humidity. Store your sneakers in a climate-controlled environment to avoid damage like yellowing or cracking.

How to Invest in Sneakers

- **Keep the Original Packaging**: The original box and packaging are part of the sneaker's value, so be sure to keep them in good condition.

How to Invest in Sneakers

Buying and Selling Sneakers

Now that you understand how to identify and secure valuable sneakers, let's look at where and how to buy and sell them.

How to Invest in Sneakers

1. Where to Buy Sneakers

There are several ways to buy sneakers for investment purposes:

How to Invest in Sneakers

- **Retail Stores and Apps**: Many limited-edition sneakers are released through the brand's official stores or apps, such as Nike's **SNKRS** app or Adidas' **Confirmed** app. These apps are your best chance of getting sneakers at retail prices.

How to Invest in Sneakers

- **Resale Platforms**: If you miss out on the initial release, you can buy sneakers on resale platforms like **StockX, GOAT, Stadium Goods**, and **Flight Club**. These platforms act as intermediaries between buyers and sellers and often authenticate sneakers to ensure they're legitimate.

How to Invest in Sneakers

- **Sneaker Conventions**: Sneaker conventions like **Sneaker Con** are great places to find rare sneakers, network with other investors, and learn more about the market.

How to Invest in Sneakers

2. How to Sell Sneakers

When it's time to sell your sneakers, you have a few options:

- **Resale Platforms**: The same platforms where you buy sneakers can also be used to sell them. StockX, GOAT, and others allow you to list your sneakers for sale, and the platform will take a small fee once the sale is complete.

How to Invest in Sneakers

- **Direct Sales**: Some investors prefer to sell directly to buyers through social media platforms like Instagram or through sneaker-focused forums like Reddit's **r/Sneakers**. This method can avoid seller fees, but it also comes with more risk, as there's no third-party authentication or protection for buyers and sellers.

How to Invest in Sneakers

- **Consignment Stores**: If you'd rather not handle the sale yourself, you can take your sneakers to a consignment store like **Flight Club** or **Stadium Goods**. These stores will sell your sneakers on your behalf and take a commission.

How to Invest in Sneakers

Risks of Sneaker Investing

While sneaker investing can be profitable, it's not without risks. Here are a few risks to keep in mind:

- **Market Volatility**: Sneaker prices can fluctuate widely based on trends, brand decisions, and cultural factors. A sneaker that's hot today might lose value tomorrow.

How to Invest in Sneakers

- **Counterfeits**: The sneaker market is rife with counterfeits, particularly for popular and expensive models. Always use trusted platforms that offer authentication services to avoid buying or selling fake sneakers.

How to Invest in Sneakers

- **Storage Costs**: Properly storing your sneakers can be costly, especially if you own a large collection. Climate-controlled storage and insurance can add up over time.

How to Invest in Sneakers

- **Liquidity Issues**: Sneakers are not as liquid as stocks or other traditional investments. It can take time to find a buyer willing to pay your asking price, especially for less popular models.

How to Invest in Sneakers

Conclusion

Sneaker investing can be a fun and profitable venture for those willing to put in the time to research the market and stay on top of trends. Understanding what drives sneaker value, how to secure rare pairs, and the best methods for selling can help you build a profitable sneaker portfolio. However, as with any investment, it's important to approach sneaker investing with caution, carefully weighing the potential risks and rewards before diving in.